THE FAR
UNKNOWN

Kingfisher Media Publishing

also by Mary Lou Kayser from Kingfisher Media

Books

Personal Branding Secrets for Beginners
If Today Was a Shape
Leadership Limericks
The Ones Who Believed

Podcast

Play Your Position

THE FAR UNLIT UNKNOWN

poems

MARY LOU KAYSER

Kingfisher Media

Published by Kingfisher Media
8630 SW Scholls Ferry Rd, #123
Beaverton, OR 97008

www.maryloukayser.com
Instagram.com/maryloukayser
LinkedIn.com/in/mlkayser

Published in the United States of America

For the man who helped me find my North Star
and proves every day there's always a ghost of a chance

Sprawling on the fringes of the city
In geometric order
An insulated border
In-between the bright lights
And the far, unlit unknown

Nowhere is the dreamer
Or the misfit so alone

— ALEX ZIVOJINOVICH
GARY LEE WEINRIB
NEIL ELWOOD PEART

We were together. I forget the rest.

— WALT WHITMAN

CONTENTS

{leaving

Harbor Song

After the snow you walk

to the water's edge

the tide is high and churning

the color of his knife

wind bites your nose

burning your cheeks raw

you look easy at the sky

and think,

This is what it means
to be American

In the park

where you spent

hours months years

of your life

walking with friends

in search of pot and beer

and a warm embrace

and maybe a face

you could fall in love with

at least for a little while

You remember this cold,

how the harbor froze

that one winter

when you walked across

to the other side and

you thought you were so cool

showing off to the boy

you loved who loved

your best friend

and you watched

as he took her hand

and not yours on the ice

Now, you walk past men

sitting in cars alone

at the water's edge

looking at porn

on their phones

and you remember

the first time you saw

a naked woman

in a magazine

you found buried

under leaves

on a path

behind the church

and your life changed

forever in that moment

when you recognized

the power she possessed

and that one day

you too would have breasts

and hair down there and

legs as long

as the highways

heading west, that you

could look into a camera

and make men come.

You knew, didn't you,

what the future held

even if nothing was clear

even if you thought

you'd rather be there

than here, that you could

run fast from everything

and everyone

on those highways

singing the harbor song,

the one you know by heart

whose music plays onward

long after you're gone

How Do You Say Goodbye to a House

Do you start room by room

Or one drawer at a time

The desk in the front hall

The workbench in the basement

Collect the shoes from the closets

Lay out the new shirts he never got to wear

Next to the ones he wore

More than forty years of binders in the attic

And all those books on trains

And cameras, watches and stars

Where is the best place to store

What you want to keep

And more importantly —

Is that even possible and if it is

Do you want to

The Making of Me Is the Breaking of Me

The making of me is the breaking of me
Or maybe it's the other way around
Another meme meant to inspire
When all it does is bring me down.

What if making wasn't breaking at all
But an ancient form of ephemeral loss where
You don't let go and toss what was and is pretty good
because of better's perennial promise.

Maybe constantly evolving and personal growth
Means you never know joy, happiness or both
From showing up just the way you are
Quietly drawn into the soft light of becoming.

Can't we linger just a little longer like a star
Meeting dawn in that soft light of becoming
Wasting time for no reason, no reason at all
A small price to pay when that softness makes us stronger.

Why is everyone in such a hurry to arrive
Somewhere they believe holds all the answers

With the filters and the shares, the likes and the stares

As if life could exist without some unpleasantness

Or the deep sadness of being because being like becoming

Isn't easy or a mouse click away.

It's not hidden within the first ten thousand fans

or data full of temporary meaning.

Being shatters expectations, drowning you in disappointment.

You gasp not from the wanting but from the weight

Of believing what could have been and what almost was

Forever haunting tomorrow's halls, that phantom atonement.

On the Day My Nephew Jumped out of a Plane

On the day my nephew jumped out of a plane

He was somewhere over Georgia for airborne training.

It was his first time and I bought new flowers.

Pansies yellow and scarlet.

Salvia in purple and pink. I bought a bag of

Edna's Best Organic Potting Soil, too,

because sometimes you pay the price to get the best.

On the day my nephew jumped out of a plane

The sun beat on the earth 92 degrees worth.

The sky the color of faded Dutch plates lining the wall on

display in a home that now echoes with the sound of tiny

voices in every room beckoning me forth.

On the day my nephew jumped out of a plane

I fought with him about money and why I didn't

believe he would come through.

He implied I did not trust him.

I said those words aren't mine, but from you.

On the day my nephew jumped out of a plane

I followed a bright orange Mustang GT on my way home

from buying new flowers and the best organic potting soil

money could buy. It turned right before I did and

I wondered what kind of person buys an orange car

and how far I could go when I know how much

he hates the color orange.

Intersection

Your dad's life is not your own

Where they intersect

Well that's interesting

Curiosity
Intelligence
Free spirited
Finer things

You keep what fits

The rest disappears

No need to hold on

To a life that's not yours

Let him go
Let him go
Let him go

Climate Change

You hate getting rid of the polar bears
and the ten reasons to travel
with Lindblad Expeditions.
Endless pages organized in binders
that once lived on dusty shelves
in your dad's study.

So you keep the photos he took
on the arctic ice, a bear pair snarling
at each other near another
positioned in downward dog,
the Wikipedia entry printed
June 29 2010 states their

conservation status as "threatened."
30 pages follow of reasons to
keep them alive and what can we do
to keep them alive?
But life is always changing,
living for awhile then dying
like arctic ice melting in
rising seas under thinning skies,

threatened by our own misdoings,

our foolish misdeeds.

Calculations that didn't add up or

were simply ignored

like the pain in his sides persisted

and he insisted it was nothing,

predictions gone awry or

simply never coming true.

Every explorer knows

you can't stop too long

at any one spot.

The ship is sailing on

to the next port where

the walruses lounge

and fart and belch.

But for this moment

you can linger

just a little longer

in these notebooks

and learn the polar bears

are okay, for now anyway.

For now you can be at peace

they are okay and maybe

one day you will see them

where he saw them, too,

from the bow of a ship

with a camera at your hip.

For now you can throw away

the walruses and keep

the polar bears,

a small act of rebellion.

The Smallest Constellation

For the longest time
you didn't let yourself dream.
Shuttered and small you
hid behind expectations
others created for you.

You want different things now
than when the rest of your life
lay ahead of you, that vast
expanse of what could be but
you couldn't possibly know.

You can't ever know what
could be, only what is right
now, this moment, and then
this. The light in the sky
looks different at dawn

than the soft purple
of late afternoon, that
magic hour when shadows
grow long and everything isn't

in focus. It's better that you

don't remember every sunrise
or noontime spread or every
word you said. Forgive and forget
lets you savor what is and what's
next as you move ahead.

You know so little about who you
are or what your life means,
only that in the long light of a day
ending you are vaguely aware of
your magnificent density, that deep

and profound knowing passed on
by those who lived before you and
in those who carry with them parts
of you, parts that one day will no
longer work but will never break.

This is what dreams are made of:
Parts that never break. A day might
be enough or you might need to
leave for a bit and come back to

the years you imagine. There's

room for that, just like there's room
for being the smallest constellation
alone with nothing to do except think
and listen to Your truest voice,
the one that doesn't shout
but whispers, you always have

A choice to make about your world
reshape it with the hands that held
your children when they were new
those same hands that love the one who
loves you, too, who offers your heart a

place among his stars. He's part
of your dream now, celestial and keen
on being what it is. Nothing more.
Eternal currency you spend wisely
from the jar he so generously offers you.

our common brutality

this is the part of the story

when I want to run

run fast and far

away and away

and then away

some more

run and run and run

I want to feel nothing

but blood pounding

in my feet

the rush of midnight

slashing my cheeks

tearing me down

my face meeting

dirt and ground

pushed so hard it will

drown out his voice

the voice

that brought me back

to life and now

whose sound

shatters me

splinters of bone

shards of my heart

splattered and tattered

sheets of my skin

torn and frayed and

whipping in the wind

and I'm gone

and I'm gone

and I'm gone

nothing but an illusion

of what I might have become

and even then

all I want to do is run

What You Weave on the Loom of Magical Thinking

You cry because you're growing

leaving behind what was

once worth knowing

or so you told yourself

back then.

A narrative you weave

on the loom of magical thinking when

for too long you didn't trust yourself,

for too long what you sensed was true

you buried behind lies and smiles

that comforted you.

To bust through those barriers now

and breathe

as if you had never taken a breath before

fuels your body, mind and heart and

through the door you're opening

into life as you've always dreamed

it could be,

shaped truly of your own accord.

You cry because out here

in the wilderness of what you desire

the stars shine brighter.

You have the strength to climb higher

and even when you fall all

it takes to rise again exists

within the deepest wells of your soul

and believing the call to lead yourself

is revealing for the first time what's

possible after tearing down

conformity's wall,

that overextended and dangerous illusion.

You cry as you say so long

to confusion, choosing to welcome and

embrace the space unfolding

into the rest of your life,

that wild garden of unconditional

surrender and purpose.

You cry because you can

and because the water

never looked so cold

or beautiful

or blue.

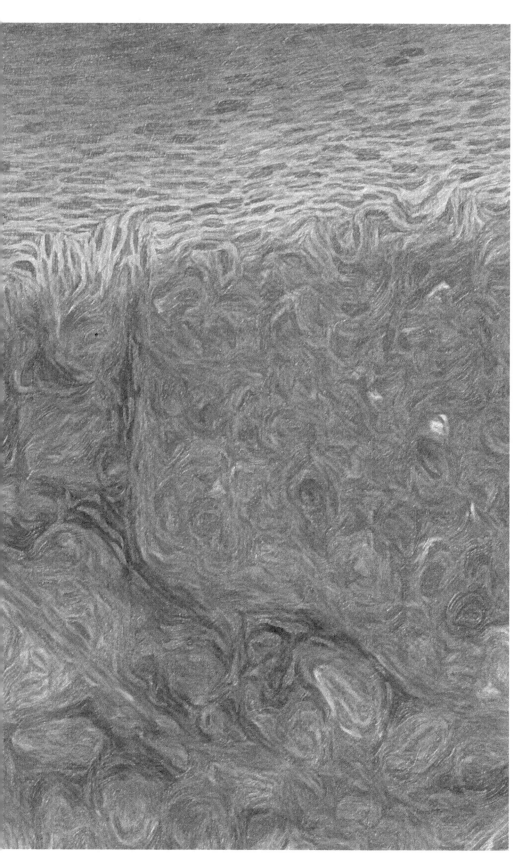

Postcards

When I was a child, my grandparents sent me
postcards from places far away.
France, Ireland, the UK,
Japan, Jerusalem, South America, Uruguay

I got postcards with tiny writing.
And I used to get such a thrill to see my name
in the address bar with a stamp.
And I thought about the places they had been,
but more often I thought about traveling myself,

Where would I go? What would I see?

I'm at a point in my life where travel and writing
are about mining memories, editing my ego,
setting aside the constant need to be in the spotlight
getting attention from people I'll never know or meet.
Now social media beats the drum in our brains
the never ending need for attention
if we are to mean anything in a world driven
by platforms we don't even own.

Meaning isn't created out of followers or likes

but from discovering those golden threads

of tiny writing, stacked in old quilts and

scattered pieces of my life in the address bar

of postcards. Forget the algorithms.

Give me a box of fading ink and ancestral dust

from places near and here and far.

No More, No Less

That time on the elementary school playground
when you fell off the swing and lost your mother's
prized sapphire ring. The one from India your
grandfather gave to her.

You didn't ask permission.

You took it from its box and slid it on your finger
admiring how it sparkled, feeling like a grown up.
Only you didn't feel so grown up when you had to confess.

It was I who took it.
It was I who lost it.
It was I, no more, no less.

Unselfing

Love

        is the extremely

           uncomfortable

difficult

                monstrous

exquisite

    thrilling

      realization

that something

          other than yourself

    is real

The lion roars when hungry

Also from pain the way that story teaches children about ferocity and the kindness that tames. How many of us walk the earth with thorns in our hearts hoping a mouse will come along and notice our frown is not anger but sadness splintered across the savanna of our parched past. We thirst for rain and a mouse to pull out the thorn and maybe our roar will become that of a satisfied lion knowing it can sleep because it has provided for its pride and its paw is no longer sore.

This Is the End of a Long Story

One conceived in a lie

That greed and lust

Pushed aside

Reckoning comes

Disguised as sunrise

You think it's just

Another day but how

Can that be after hands

Tongues, screams, sighs

This is when you pray

For rain gushing from

Heavy clouds, the release

Is painful and sweet

You held in so long

Too long until you had

Nowhere else to go

Standing outside that door

In the rain, the bottle of wine

Half drunk you cradled

Between your thighs

Driving like someone else

How could you have been

Yourself when you thought

You knew, when you believed

The story his lips told you

As he lay with his hands

Behind his head

Insulting in its casual pose

While you cried in his bed

Because he made you

Feel beautiful and said

Go home to your children

Be the magnificent mother

They call for when they're sick

Or excited because the

Smell of fall is kissing

Their noses with a promise

and the roses along

the fence are still red

el viajero fantomo

ghost rider in the wind

rapids raging through your heart

soul's alight with fire and love

burning bright straight from the start

ghost rider on river north

pounding steel inside your chest

around the bend a canyon full

among the trees a place to rest

ghost rider blazing fast

a mile ahead of the setting sun

another day within your grasp

you'll make the most of this next one

ghost rider before the storm

gather dust and rain and bone

fill your coffers, bare your soul

ride you must this ride alone

for Neil Peart

grieving}

The Great Undoing

Crumpled on the top shelf

of your dad's closet

a pair of Carhartt's

in their signature

butterscotch brown, stiff

unwashed and new

size 42

too small for him and

you know they are too big for you

You try them on anyway

because they were your dad's

and because overalls are cool

the way his chamois shirts

you wore in high school were cool

Your dad said goodbye to size

42 long ago. Still — he held on to this pair

the way some women keep size eight jeans

next to the fourteens for masochistic inspiration

and to remember who they once were

they know damn well those days

are gone forever and

it's okay to have a dream

Believing is what matters

that one day you could look

in the mirror knowing everything

you now know to be true

about yourself and the way it works

without crumpling under the weight

of the great undoing and your dad

is gone and so are many of the things

you once loved and that once loved you

There will be days when you will want

to shove what's too big into drawers

or hide them on top of unwashed shelves

crumpled, stiff, unwashed, new

But you won't

You will get dressed

You will get dressed again

and again

and again

because getting dressed says

you're still here

and there are more days ahead

and more clothes to wear

Head West

I love you but I like you more

I don't know how to do this

Love and all that jazz

Peeling back the layers

Exposing the tender underbelly

Of my soul

Letting someone in

Letting someone see the realest me

They get too close and I run

Fast and hard toward the setting sun

Head west head west where

The rest of my life waits

Break me open before I'm done

The Summer I Wore Long Earrings

The summer I wore long earrings

And short skirts

We read the Myth of Sisyphus by Camus.

I told you about teaching the Greek version

The original, how one boy named Jason

Who loved Galileo and the Quadratic equation

Wanted to argue with me

about the sheer implausibility

of a man rolling the same rock

Up the same hill every day

For the rest of eternity

Even if he had been punished by the Gods.

You smiled because it was the right thing to do

Unlike what we did in Sacramento

In that park by the oak tree

Its bony roots under me

With you and its canopy above

Your face as round as the moon

Stars or no stars, rising, rising in my heart

There it was when I looked out my window

Big and bold in the growing dark of sky.

If I could have reached my hand into that gulf

Between us, pushed down the moon and

Stopped it from rising, rising, always rising

I never would have tasted the salt of your

Ideas about what could be true, or your tongue,

A smoldering coal of what would never come.

Remembering

What else do we have

But this moment

Now this one

And this

And all those we store

In boxes on shelves in the garage

Under the bed in airtight bags

I told myself when I read out loud
Foxie
Where the Wild Things Are
Babar and Celeste

I promised myself I would remember

Those moments

That I would always

Make those moments last

If only I could make those

Moments last

With small warm bodies

Nestled next to me

The sound of sleep falling gently

Into the gathering dark

I stayed longer there than I needed to

Because in those moments

Of small voices with big intentions

Striped pajamas and coming down

Stairs on Christmas morning

There were hands to hold on to

It meant something

I was still someone

Your Words Are Hot in My Mouth

Your words are hot in my mouth
The way the woods were hot that night

My tongue stained bright, strawberry
Red like Starbursts in the back

Of the limo, sticky, sweet, lingering
A beat too long

June comes, then August heat
Clouds hijacked July

I waited for water to fall from the sky
And I waited for you to call but that

Well had run dry and then
September came and settled

In my bones like a song I can't forget
and still, no rain

After You Delete Instagram off Your Phone

After you delete Instagram off your phone
You find a different kind of sadness inside
The folder named "social," a sadness
That lingers long after returning the phone
To its charging cradle next to your desk.

Your finger now has nowhere to go
When you're looking for ways to escape
The self-hatred and loathing that comes
From comparing. What is so social anyway
About staring at a screen the size of an
Angry fist hoping someone somewhere
With a huge list and an underscore in their name
Likes your latest selfie, the one where the wind
Blows your hair across your face, catching you
By surprise, your shirt dark in places with sweat?

You'd get more out of staring into the
Pond in the sump at the end of the street
Where frogs perform nightly their symphony
Of sweet longing and desire in a low throaty baseline

A fine reminder that you still look good, you do,

Don't you? Especially against that sky dark blue

How good the scene with its valleys

And expanse of river so few listen to as it tells

The story about a world so enormous we can barely

Imagine how it originally formed us into the tiny

Pixels receding ever slightly one fragment at a time

Into its milky marbled background where no confetti falls

From the ceiling or trophies line empty halls.

I write the words I want to say and you don't want to hear

They tumble onto the page
like newborn cubs rolling on the ground
before instinctively searching
to suckle from their mother's breast

I long to hold your hand and tell you
to rest, at least for the afternoon
but I stop the words before they leave my head
the gate comes up, the moat gets filled

and I stay silent yet again

Before You Can Continue

Before you can continue

You need to provide your birthday

We need to know

You aren't too young

Or too old

(We're guessing you're probably too old)

Although we can't say that

Not legally

The boundaries of age

Are thicker when you're young

Not yet ready to see

The photos side by side

What's real and highly subsidized

Through masks

And filters

And what's that on her head

And no one — not even supermodels —

Look that good in bed

Before you can continue

You need to check in with yourself

Are you in good health

And are you in touch with the way

It is in the real world with

The tears and the scars and

The endless parade of broken hearts

We need to know

You won't go blow the whistle

On what really goes on around here

The smoke and mirrors and that

Small little man behind the curtain

We don't want you to see or hear

Before you can continue

You need to agree to the new

Terms and conditions determining

Your experience

They're not what you think they are

But then is anything

So there's that

That one tiny knob controlling your brain defining

everything

You see and then believe you saw

No really it was there you swear

You saw the light around his hair

And her face and the place

You used to go when you didn't yet know

It wouldn't work out

The way the photos show

The sun won't last

And you'll be again alone

In heartbreak's basement

Where long dark shadows

live and grow

Infinity

For a moment,

you will understand infinity

in the ferns unfurling

and the smell of dirt

after it rains.

You weren't looking for it

or maybe you were

and the words hadn't

come to you yet.

Maybe that's what it means

to give yourself permission to

run your hands through the muck

of grief's monstrous underbelly

the gritty darkness can do you good

the endless expanse of nothing.

Maybe you will focus on endings

which turn into beginnings

instead of always chasing

what's new and maybe

an ending isn't all that bad,

a path forward into

the light of becoming and

a call to be your most honest

and true since who you are

is never as far from being real

as steel to a car or the edge

of a knife or the sky

clearing blue after a storm

passes through. Now you can

see. Yes. It's like that too.

For a moment

maybe that's what you'll do

Dream the dream onward

when no one's looking

when you can give away everything

without feeling farewell's sting.

Be the fern unfurling.

Liturgy

If song carries away some of the ache of sorrow,

what do words do?

Can a preposition heal a wounded heart

over time

through the process

moving *on*

beyond fear and doubt

Is a noun the answer to the question loss asks:

What is *grief, Love,*

and how about *gratitude*

Tears work, too, and *vespers*

Is the secret hidden in an adjective

disarming

intuitive

generous

Maybe the only way home is in the arms of a verb

shoulder
sob
weep
bear witness
deliver us from evil

forgive

good men with guns

good men with guns
took down a bad man
in France who killed
85 people with his truck

dead

good men with guns
stop bad men
unless bad men
fool good men with guns

stand down
hold your fire
wait

on sidewalks and platforms
we broadcast our sorrow
we speak of purple mountains majesty
and amber waves of grain

what about the endless waves
of blood and grief

crashing into schools

crushing our souls

rivers of red

washing across a nation

that now mourns

21 more people

dead

and tomorrow, four

and the next day, more

there are more good men

with guns than bad

good men

who sacrifice their lives

dead

for family
for fairness
for freedom

not for revenge or hate

or because they were bullied

when they were eight

but because

good men with guns

love their country and appreciate

what We once all believed

one Nation
under God
indivisible

we must do a better job

and stop good men with guns

from having to lay down their lives

for all that's at stake

if we don't then our fate

is divided we fall

right now that writing is

too loud on the wall

we can do this, America

stand united, arms linked

proud and tall

good men with guns

pledge allegiance to liberty

and justice for all

Trees Part I

There's something about trees in winter.

When they are without leaves, silhouetted against steel skies
and the air as sharp as a new blade.

They wave and bend, standing strong against the wind
roaring down from the north,

harsh conditions and yet exposed without their foliage.

That's what makes them beautiful.

Strength originates in the seeds of vulnerability,

Immune to the fiercest storms that will bring you to your
knees

When your mind isn't right

When you've lost sight of the richness and texture and depth

Just like the raw unexpected beauty of winter trees

We see what we choose to see, ignorant or consciously.

{loving

Before the Storm

You roll onto each other's shore
Parched and close to drowning
Tossed out of the storm that raged
Deep in the cage of longing.

Here, it says. *See if you can make it one
more time.* That's what love does,
after all, isn't it? Grants you that
one more time you hand your tender

heart to another and say, *Here.*
See if you can hold this. It's been broken
before so don't worry if you drop it
on the floor. Over the years it's become

a door without a lock, the key long
since forgotten at the back of a dusty drawer.
Over the years you've learned
Love's Truth will be in the first kiss and you

can't break love or punch it down with
your fist. Glass and bones, crowns and

thrones will shatter under malice's weight

but not love. Love burns hate and

takes down rage and clears away the

storms with one strike of its match,

precision so exact you wonder how you

could have once ignored the thunder

rolling through your heart. It wasn't as

much of a warning as the start of your

Love story growing, the one you tell now

from the shore before the storm, the one

and only one worth writing as your own.

The Far Unlit Unknown

The slender thread

that stitched you together

is woven into the space

between silence and sound

and the quilt

you lie under

after you become one

not knowing where

the other ends

and you begin

in the far unlit unknown

If it were a guitar,

its notes would carry

beyond the walls

of a music hall

or the radio broadcasting

a timeless tune

tapping memories

both ancient and new

If it were a color

it would be alto blue

like the sky

just after twilight and rain

and without a moon.

On nights like that

you can see stars

being born when

the milky way lays

gently across the dark

and you gaze in wonder

as you're pulled

further under

and ask if it's possible

to be this happy

and ask:

Is it possible to share

a sense of deep

aliveness and pay attention

to the world together

where you make

visible life's invisibles

extending kindness

to everything

within and without.

When you take

each other's hands

gone is any doubt

that this splendid surprise

belongs to you

and how wise are you to

say yes, yes, yes

in its rush

of gentle commands

and how prescient

to agree that

this, this, this

is what it means

to surrender

as woman

as love

as man

Pauses

You think of a random question
to ask the next time he calls

Do you think Indians cry
when they remember their dead?

Or do they move ahead
along with the seasons

knowing the reasons
for life and death
are one and the same?

You want to know
Does he cry

and when and why
if it's from the memory

of your skin
or how you taste

is that enough to bring

a smile

a tear

a pause

to his face

what is life after all

but moments between pauses

when everything falls into place

including the causes

and it's just the two of you

side-by-side

not knowing

if it's the end of the day

or the beginning of the night

Two Is One

You talk about our chemistry

And the physics of us

$e = mc$ squared

that this is fate

As universal as Newton's Law

The force that increases

with mass and decreases

exponentially with distance

And you laugh because

Laughing soothes

The ride your heart's

Been on faster than

any bike or truck you've owned.

How could we have known

I would discover you

watching me watching you,

fate + faith lets us see

the truth about

Possibility, and we agree

Our first kiss eradicated

eternal loneliness

fingers entwined

Where we knew they always

Belonged. To miss one second

akin to blasphemy. Instead

We choose reverence and piety

Elements of our chemistry

When you talk about us

One is none and two is one

The only way love gets done

The Things We Found Out

And in the middle

of the most

ferocious storm

you wrote poems

about loss

and about love

about climbing and

standing still

about running the rapids

when you were young

You wrote poems until

you didn't think you had

another one

and then another

showed itself and

you said, Yes.
Please ride with me this way.

You hear the quiet

in your mind of Alaska

from the ridge of tundra

and the lake at night

and the sun

rising over the trees

the smell of snow and

the wind and him

inside of you

It keeps you breathing,

enough for today

This is the hard

part of love

after the fall

you land not gracefully

on your feet

the way the

movies make

love out to be

but in a rumpled

mess of limbs and

leaves tangled in

cords and the knots

growing in trees

and the roots

of your heart

The easy part

is at the start

when you don't know,

when you don't know

how you'll feel or

what sounds

you'll hear

or why when you

leave for the night

and all you did was

run your fingers across

the warm surface

of his beat

before resting gently

on his arm

You allow that river to

continue running

through you

long after you're gone

that river of lust

and heat

and love

and song

leads you to what has

always been true

about the one

you didn't expect

to meet

And of course

you met because

that's how love works

the work of love

is what you do with

your hands

under the blanket

he keeps

in your spot

on the couch

and you watch

what he likes

about bikes and knives

and trucks and gear,

and you hear

what he does

when he's alone

in the woods

processing the wild

with his ax

and the tactical lantern

that burns through

the night and

the assurance of firelight

close to his tent

You went fast and deep

and sense this one

can last because

you know who

you are and

loving another may

be hard

or it could be

the easiest thing

you find, spending

your time

for the rest

of your life

Love could be

the most obvious yes

at the river's bend

where the best

rapids run through

your canyon

to the end

Looks Like You Didn't Have Any Writing Activity Last Week

Maybe that's because

all my activity was

tied up in fucking

and not turning a phrase

or crafting a suite

of subject lines

or putting down

whatever fleeting thoughts

might have come to mind

given how all that fucking

set sail to my thoughts

beyond my body and his

fingers tongue and

circumnavigating

miles and miles

of skin basking

in the sun

of two lovers

paying attention

to nothing

but the other

so no

I didn't have any

writing activity last week

and gauging by the look

in his eyes and the dance

between our thighs

most likely

won't again this week

and oh how so

very happy and

preoccupied am I

Good Parts

Let's fast forward to the good parts
skip ahead past the lengthy
drawn out introductions in big bold font
the gladhanding

the saccharine smiles and superficial small talk
heavy with questions about why we're here
and what do we want from this experience
We know why we're here and what we want

To get to the good parts

where we go deep and wide
with words that matter and sometimes without
none of this how are you and hi
Fast forward then rewind again and again to the good parts

Wear out the tape and the grooves in our favorite song
The one on the album laying next to the bed
Whose liner notes we've memorized
That song we can't get out of our head

Fast forward to the good parts, ya

Sing the soundtrack of our favorite movie until we're dead

Forget Lucy and Ricky

I'll be Ethel and you'll be Fred

They spent a lot of time romping around in their bed

Exactly where we belong

The good parts, ya

When we say everything is temporary

We mean only the bad parts

The good parts never need to end

A dangerous place to be when you hear really good news

The side of a cliff

The beach in a storm

5 o'clock traffic

You want to believe

What you hear

will last. These days

the news is often so bad

To hear something good

and to know you could feel

like this for far longer

than you ever have

is hard to believe

like the way he holds

your hands when

he's on top of you

Like the light in his eyes

when he's remembering

the campfire and his tent

and the vast blanket

of darkness dotted with stars

and the smell of trees

and water moving

on the wind

through his wilderness

Time Blocking

The moments we spend

Touching

Talking

Saying nothing at all

With words

And everything

We have ever wanted

to say with

Skin and tongues

Aren't color coded blocks

Scheduled between the inbox

And Zoom meetings

And endless tasks to do

No

Our river of time flows

Down from the mountains

Of zero expectations

Into the valley of

A surprise afternoon

And a look

And a glance

And a smile shared

When we agree

At the exact same time

How bad the chicken is and

The sushi is okay

And what's even more okay

Is how good my ass looks

In those jeans and your eyes

And our knees brush

Under the table and

The heat

      The heat

            The heat

Status

My status says

I'm married to

no one

In a relationship with

no one

It can be lonely

being married to

And in a relationship with

no one

Once

it would be nice

To see my status say

Married to

Or in a relationship with

Someone

Not just myself

Or I

Or me

But the man

with a name who

Captured my heart

And let me see

What can happen

When one man truly loves

One woman

His Queen

Her King

Their everything

Not afraid of being seen

Holding up their crowns

With both middle fingers

Because who the fuck cares

What your status shows or

Who you love

Or when or why

Or whether you're married

Or in a relationship by

Your own choosing

Because that's what together

you decided to do

With the love

you give him

And the love

he so kindly

gives to you

When I Was in School

When I was in school AIDS was a gay man's disease

Still a mystery to most and taught with unease

Given all of the others that sounded horrific

how terrific I believed one wasn't as cruel.

Two of my favorite teachers were gay.

One would say I had the photographer's eye

which I took as a compliment

Because that's how he meant it.

The other said I reminded him of Jane Fonda

He suggested I wanted to be just like her.

AIDS would get him in the end but not the other

who suffered an aneurysm.

He did not recover. I have photos of both men in

Different places. On a boat, on the beach their faces

As wide as a child's smile on Christmas morning

Unwrapping presents and gobbling down treats.

How sweet to meet their goodness

Thirty years later as I remember

what every one of my teachers can claim.

"We were part of what made her."

But those two put most of the others to shame

when I was in school. They got me, you see,

beyond the external. Something not quite paternal

I loved all the same.

Freedom's Currency

I don't paint murals

To save the bees

I don't dig holes

To plant the trees

I don't buy pencils

To help build schools

I don't buy into

Other people's rules

About how to give

And what it's like

To support the causes

To be in the fight

I give my love

Unconditionally

In words on the page

Freedom's currency

being}

How to Become a Poet

It might begin

with Peter and the Wolf

on the floor of the living room,

pawing your chubby hands

across the spines

of your dad's albums

lined precisely in rows

The sound of the cello

and the flute

rising to meet

the deep throated oboe

and violin

Or it could be the way

your dad ran his whiskers

across your cheeks

when he kissed you good night

and you burrowed down deep

under covers so tight

where it was warm and safe,

the light in the hall gently

fading from sight

Maybe it comes from the hum

of your mother sewing

you and your brother

new clothes for school,

the Mets game on the radio

and the roar of her cheers

and the fans

and the concession men

selling them beers

Perhaps it was

your third grade teacher

who liked the gerbil

you described in a poem

you wrote that then

won you a prize

Sometimes it comes

from somewhere outside

but most often you'll find

it comes from within

when you give yourself permission

to not just listen

but imagine

what a girl sees each morning

who wakes up in Tibet

and what the lion tastes

when his teeth are

covered with blood

and what the man you let enter

the deepest sanctuary of your soul

finds in that soft sacred place

beyond your tongue

and your ass

and your face

because how could anyone believe

letting someone in

makes you weak

when the opposite is true

Beyond the mere mortal,

it's a shuttle to the eternal

where the window reveals

what life has in store for you

and it's no surprise to notice

so much more left to learn

and dream with him and feel

What I'm Made of

I have known rage and worn its fiery robes

I have known the quiet after it snows

I've spoken in tongues no one understands

I've held children close with gentle hands

Rage is by far the one I know best

It rises from a place deep in my chest

And howls for attention and someone to love

Rage knows exactly what I'm made of

Pending Tasks

Temporary satisfaction

from marking complete

those tasks on your list

Drawing a line through

what you deem important

on that day

That line etched with extra

emphasis says done

in a way nothing else can

A certain kind of freedom.

What do pending tasks

reveal about what you

believe is too beautiful

or maybe not as important

as you told yourself

when you wrote them down?

What happens if you never

draw a line through

Assemble photo collage
Fill bird feeders
Clean walls in tower for paint prep
Say "I love you" right out loud

Will you be able

to mark your life complete

feeling satisfied

or will never getting around

to feeding the birds

and saying I love you

leave a scar thicker

and more sinister

on your heart than

the thin blue line

you would scratch

across the back of

the grocery receipt

marking complete

what you prioritized

as important on that day

Would it say

Finished
Over
Done
Opportunity missed
Gone for good

Or could it be that

maybe some tasks

repeat indefinitely

and it's never too late

Marking Time

The day will come when

no one counts your followers

or how many brand pillars you built

The cardinal at my feeder

this morning certainly doesn't.

Nor will her offspring

or their offspring or

the offspring after that.

The owl won't howl

if no one notices it perched

in the tree above the wetland.

Attention is the last thing it craves.

All the fuss about the latest IPO

or algorithm reconfiguration

fades to black when you discover

a nest out back with three

speckled blue eggs and the return

of the ruby throated hummingbirds.

The blackberries this summer will grow
bearing fruit so succulent and fat
you'll be full after clearing one long branch
trailing into the grass, your lips and fingers
stained the color of a giraffe's tongue.

You won't worry about blood
on your shirt where thorns
dug into your flesh marking time,
marking time as it has for centuries
long before you arrived.

Always the Bride

You're not the obvious choice

And certainly not their first

When they enter the room

You don't shove your boobs

In their face or

Flutter fake eyelashes

Beckoning them to

Head in your direction

You don't follow

their erection

To the bathroom and

Let them do to you

What they see when

They're alone

with their phone

You sit quietly

in the non-obvious zone

thinking and knowing

Laughing and watching

them fall down hard

The same rabbit hole

With the same dead end

And you know, you know

The smart ones will eventually

Find their way home to you and

You know when they do

you will let them in

You will open the door and they

Will tell you they wonder what

took them so long to come to you,

why were they so dumb

Not to notice who was there

All along, the obvious choice

You with your voice and your

Face and your mind, the kind

Of woman they want to

Make their bride.

They discover what's inside

matters most. You forgive them

And never forget

It's not easy not being

The obvious choice or their first

It's your blessing and your curse

No regrets

You're different and that's okay

You wouldn't want it

Any other way

A Briefcase Full of Pencils

A briefcase full of pencils

Sits on a shelf in the back

of the front hall closet

Pressed between a wall

And the stack of puzzles

Still waiting to be built

Dust covers every surface

And I sneeze and I remember

Hiding in this closet

When I was a girl

Hoping someone would

Miss me and then come looking

And also hoping I could hide

Behind coats and escape

Forever into the stories

Of the people who once

Wore them

We can only speak of new stories

And not look to the past

For what we most desire

But with one hand shading

Our eyes, gaze into the vastness

of what is becoming, that which

Our hearts are drawn toward

The magnet of possibility

Keeps the lights on and lets

Us swing our legs out of bed

One more morning and maybe

this is the day when everything

we dream about shows itself

And confirms our longings

Aren't mere wishes but as

Predictable as a flower unfolding

Along the shores of a ferocious

And magnanimous ocean

And a briefcase full of pencils

Alongside puzzles full of hope

Shadow World

You were born into a world

You're no longer living in

That world is gone

Even if much of it looks

The same. Oceans roil and

Rain falls and the sun comes

Up in the morning.

But this is not your shadow

World before a man stepped

Onto the moon and people

Wrote letters and met and

Fell in love without an algorithm

And didn't talk back to each other

Or make their own news.

The war on a virus doesn't hold

Us together the way the wars

Against madness and oppression

Generated conversations ripe with

Meaning and purpose. Chasing

Likes on the surface seems to

Hold a big promise but loses its

Shine the second it's posted.

Don't scroll away your life

Or believe what you see

Is the way it's always

Been or always will be.

Trust me — so much

More awaits you away

From the tiny screen

In a world that isn't the

World you were

Born into but has every

Opportunity to become

What you imagine it can be.

A river swollen with possibilities

Full of love

Full of light

That world is worth the fight

To make it real and

To seal for yourself

What you know is true

The world can be better

Because of what you choose

To think and feel and do.

Feathering a Stick

It's like finding yourself

When you learn

Your heritage

When you learn

Your lineage

When you see

For the first time

Your curly, unfurling line

Scattered on the ground

Shavings of the past

Offer heat for the night

Promise light for the future

Yours and Yours Alone

Your life is yours

And yours alone

Just as the sun's heat

Is not the moon's

The Kenai can't be

the Amazon or the Rhône

You were slow to know

These things

Moving more like water

In a delta than the burst

Of a river's first stream

So set on getting to where

It was destined to go

Yours has been a more

Roundabout path

Following unorthodox

Curves in the road

A bend here, an angle there

Mileposts measured by
Adventures and men
Who captured your heart
until the roll of your water
pulls you to start
another leg of your

Journey, the one only
You can feel and hear
and taste and see and own
Rushing over boulders
Smoothing down stones
Etching memories deep

Down in your bones
More like the Kenai
Than the Amazon
or the Rhône
Your life is yours
and yours alone

The Center of Things

When I first found myself in the center of things
I heard no fanfare such events can bring

No red carpet or glitter lay under my feet
No presidents or Kings was I scheduled to meet

The gown you might think that I would have worn
wasn't yet designed or sewn. But what had been born

was a sense of completeness with the way of the world
something I'd sensed had been missing since I was a girl.

Finding myself in the center of things
meant shutting out voices and commands so my wings

Could take me from places they'd created and wanted
while the life I was seeking for myself haunted

the halls of each day that I lived in the Lie
of what others believed were the rules to live by

But they are as trapped and confused as the rest
unable to shake years of others knowing best

What's best for them isn't best for me
when the passion came along it forced me to free

myself from those ropes tied around my legs
It teased and cajoled and screamed and begged

"Your life is your own! You must live it your way!"
In the center of things I no longer fall prey

to the turmoil that rolls into chasms out there
Deep among those who sincerely believe that they care

about me and my life but they don't, not a whit
they care only for power, their own, lots of it

yet the power they seek over me is in them
True authentic power only comes from within

When I know what I'm doing in the world is right
despite all the protests and challenges and fights

When I follow my heart to see what it brings
It always leads me home to the center of things

Trees Part II

Herman Hesse believed trees are our greatest teachers

Telling us something about ourselves

Revealing leaf by leaf and bough by bough

Twisted branches and so many knots

The wonder of our roots

The splendor of being human

No matter the season we turn and grow toward the sun

In storms we bend, reaching out and down

Naked and not afraid, grafting strength from the forest

And, if we happen to stand alone

Given time, our grace grounds us,

ready to bloom again in the face of friable expectations,

sprouting a new chapter in

the foliage of our glorious, self-salving overstory

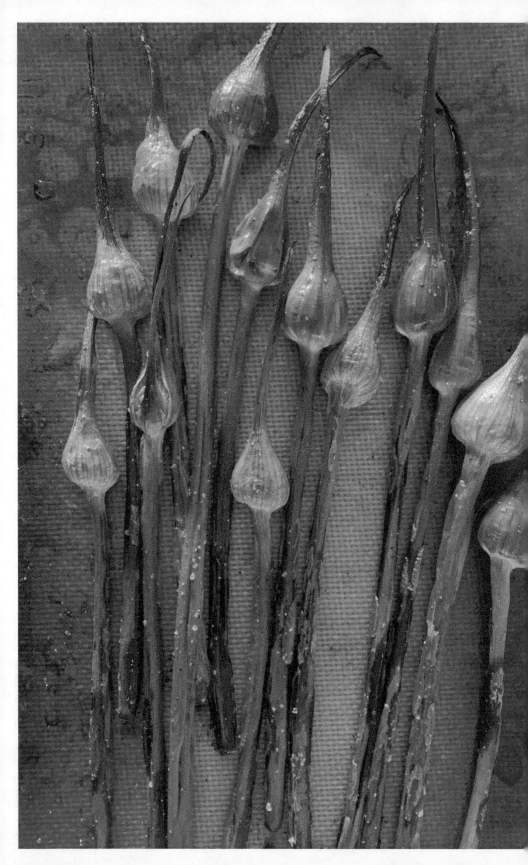

What Are You Doing

Is the line in the mirror

You ask alone

Combinations of clothes

On the bed render

A blurry background

What you are doing

Requires no answer

To address what's bold

Serves no purpose

You are doing what

Right now makes sense

Maybe not tomorrow

And yesterday was too soon

Doing what you are

Doing because the heart

Wants what it wants

And you can't stop the heart

With a question nor declare

What you are doing

Has no place in this life

The only life you know

When you are doing what

Keeps alive Desire's dare

walking through two worlds at the same time

I have never

been this happy

I never knew it was

possible to be

this happy

to feel this good

to feel like

the world has

wrapped its giant

pillow arms around

me and is kissing

the top of my head

saying,

you will never be
afraid or that lonely
again

NOTES

The book's title and poem "The Far Unlit Unkown" is named for a line in the song "Subdivisions" by RUSH, which appeared on their 1982 album, *Signals.*

When Neil Peart traveled across Mexico on his motorcycle, he signed the letters he wrote to his friend Bruno during that trip, *"El viajero fantomo."*

A line in the poem "The Far Unlit Unknown" references an article by Maria Popova on her blog, The Marginalian: "Mary Oliver on What Attention Really Means and Her Moving Elegy for Her Soul Mate."

A few words about the poem, "Good Men with Guns." I am sensitive to the conversation currently happening in the United States regarding fire arms. Regardless of where our personal beliefs fall on the continuum, there is a shared sense of collective grief over the rising number of mass shootings which is why I ultimately included the poem in this collection. Grief is often thought of as a private, individual experience. I wanted to explore what collective grief might sound like while recognizing that there are more good people -- men and women -- who own guns responsibly. As of the publication of this book, the number of mass shootings in America for 2022 is 532. This is 532 too many.

Mary Lou Kayser is a writer, teacher, podcaster, maker of poems, mom, budding toy and game designer, and ginormous sports fan who loves watching football and baseball and has been known to cheer for the Cinderella teams during March Madness. She also enjoys a good match-up during the Stanley Cup playoffs. Mary Lou has loved writing and words since she held a pencil for the first time, probably around age four. She currently lives in an 1895 Victorian on the Gold Coast of Long Island where she is reconnecting with her New York roots. When she isn't in New York, Mary Lou enjoys spending time in the Pacific Northwest where she raised her two children, and on a lake in Maine where her family has been vacationing every summer since 1969.

ACKNOWLEDGMENTS

My deepest gratitude to:

Family & Friends

Jim & Mary Grace Lyman

Ginna Kayser

Ben Kayser

Rob & Sue Lyman

Renee Simas

Jill Lopez

Margaret Bowles

Melissa Bauer

Laura Noel

Elevate Your Expertise

Angela Talbott

Dawn Stith

Diane Gibson

Confluence

Tracy Imm

Traci Esteve

Heidi Piper

Drunk Moles

Lawrence Fielding

Valentin P. Castillou

Robert Cretu

Nadia Liapi

Vinod Thomas

Diane Law

D.J. King

Gaynor Johnson

Sales and the City

Chris Miller

Amy Bobchek

Jennifer Griffin

Geri Ann Higgins

Anya Krebs

Adi Klevit

Angela McTammany

Susan Perry

Kokua Technologies

Jeff Platt

Kelly Lyons